I0605258

Advance Praise for *Sharing the Light*

"What a luminous and generous book! In these pages, Monique Gray Smith shares five timeless ways of being—gratitude, love, joy, happiness, and hope. With her signature warmth and wisdom, she guides us in discovering how to nurture these qualities and 'bring light' into every circumstance of our lives, illuminating paths toward resilience, creativity, and increased human connection." —ELIZABETH GILBERT, bestselling author of *Eat, Pray, Love*

"*Sharing the Light* by Monique Gray Smith feels like an invitation to the kitchen table to share a pot of tea with a beloved auntie. Her tender words and heartfelt stories provide gentle guidance to remind us how we can care for each other and ourselves, with attention to the profound power of small acts. Monique's reflections celebrate the gift economy of kindness, which softens the sharp edges of our lives and nourishes the bonds among us." —ROBIN WALL KIMMERER, bestselling author of *Braiding Sweetgrass*

"The first word in *Sharing the Light* is tawâw, Cree for welcome, but more deeply understood to mean there is always room in our hearts. This small book is big on tawâw. It's roomy and full of windows to let in the light we carry. It is generative, engaging, and illuminating. Monique tells us Love is Medicine. For the love and medicine that is this book, I will keep *Sharing the Light* close by as a guide to a good life." —SHELAGH ROGERS, founding host and co-creator, *The Next Chapter*, CBC Radio; chancellor, Queen's University

Sharing the Light

Stories and Reflections

Monique Gray Smith

AMBROSIA

Published in Canada and the USA in 2026 by House of Anansi Press Inc.
houseofanansi.com

House of Anansi Press is committed to protecting our natural environment. This book is made of material from well-managed FSC®-certified forests, recycled materials, and other controlled sources.

House of Anansi Press is a Global Certified Accessible™ (GCA by Benetech) publisher. The e-book version of this book meets stringent accessibility standards and is available to readers with print disabilities.

30 29 28 27 26 1 2 3 4 5

Library and Archives Canada Cataloguing in Publication

Title: Sharing the light : stories and reflections / Monique Gray Smith.
Names: Gray Smith, Monique, 1968- author
Identifiers: Canadiana (print) 2025024893X |
Canadiana (ebook) 20250248956 | ISBN 9781487013547 (hardcover) |
ISBN 9781487013554 (EPUB)
Subjects: LCSH: Self-actualization (Psychology) |
LCSH: Gratitude. | LCSH: Love. | LCSH: Happiness. |
LCSH: Hope. | LCSH: Gray Smith, Monique, 1968-
Classification: LCC BF637.S4 G733 2026 | DDC 158.1—dc23

Jacket and interior design: Alysia Shewchuk
Jacket artwork: *Dragonfly* by Betty Albert

House of Anansi Press is grateful for the privilege to work on and create from the Traditional Territory of many Nations, including the Anishinabeg, the Wendat, and the Haudenosaunee, as well as the Treaty Lands of the Mississaugas of the Credit.

Canada Council for the Arts
Conseil des Arts du Canada

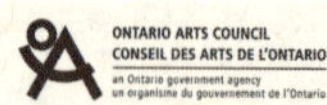

With the participation of the Government of Canada
Avec la participation du gouvernement du Canada | Canada

We acknowledge for their financial support of our publishing program the Canada Council for the Arts, the Ontario Arts Council, and the Government of Canada.

Printed and bound in Canada

For my parents, Ed and Shirley Smith,
who each in their own way taught me about
the importance of gratitude, love, joy,
happiness, and hope.

And for my family, Rhonda, Jaxson,
and Sadie, thank you for bringing
such beautiful light to my life.

Contents

Tawâw

Tawâw (ta-WOW) means welcome in Cree, but it means more than that; it also means there is always room. To me, this is what sharing the light is about—ensuring there is always room in our hearts, minds, and spirits to create, share, and receive light. Sometimes, I think welcoming light into our lives is an act of courage. Yes, an act of courage. If you think about the times in your life when there has been immense darkness—maybe you are even in one of those times right now—the darkness requires us to be vulnerable and receive tender care from either someone or some being sharing their light with us. Or it requires us to figure out how to generate our own light.

Our light is our inner wisdom, divinity, and hope shining a path forward for ourselves, and sometimes others. The more light we generate and receive, the more access we have to our imagination, dreams, ideas, possibilities, and hope!

I'm sure you've all had the experience when you meet someone and there is just something special about them. You feel changed from being around them, you notice you have more energy, perhaps you feel more optimistic and inspired. They are sharing their light.

Perhaps you have also had the opposite experience, when you meet or spend time around someone and you leave their presence with stooped shoulders, lower energy, and the day feeling a bit more difficult. For me, negativity, judgment, harshness, and mean-spiritedness usually cause me to close in on myself and protect my light.

Although we can generate and share light, there are also times when we need to protect our light. We do not have to share our light with everyone. Let me say that again. *We do not have to share our light with everyone.* We can choose who we share our light with. This is not about being better than or alienating someone. Instead, this is a conscious decision to care for ourselves and the light we carry. I especially find this important when my light is a mere flicker. I cannot give away the oxygen that keeps my flicker burning.

To remove ourselves from a situation, to leave a person's presence, to end a call, or to stop the text thread—or even end a relationship or friendship—might not be an easy or popular decision. Rather it is a beautiful practice of love—love for yourself, and love for the other person to ensure we don't feel resentful or engage in martyrdom. This doesn't mean we necessarily cut that person out of our life. Perhaps they need someone to share light with them, but you don't always have to be the one.

Receiving the Light We Need

In September 2023, I woke up with an idea. As I sat up in bed and my feet hit the floor, I felt like a three-year-old—energized, eager, and excited for the day. I love ideas and am always grateful for them, as they feel like gifts. This one felt extra special because it was wrapped in joy. The idea was to host a four-part video series called *Sharing the Light*. For each episode, I'd visit with an incredible human who would share some of their life's journey—times when they needed to receive light from others, times when they were the ones sharing light, and how they fostered their own light in difficult times.

I reached out to the four prospective guests and heard back from all of them within half an hour—Yes! They were on board. This felt like a sign that the idea had positive, vibrant momentum.

So the planning, organizing, and promotion began … with a thud! Although there was a lot of interest on social media, ticket sales were slow (and that's being generous). I was curious about the reasons why. Was the timing bad? Had my intuition led me astray? Had I priced us out of the market? These questions led to more questions, which led to uncertainty and doubt.

Around the same time, I shared a meal with Lisa, a dear friend of more than thirty-five years. When you have been friends with someone that long, you have witnessed the fullness of each other's lives—the triumphs, heartbreaks, doubts, relationships, adventures, and misadventures. I told her about how things were not unfolding with the video series as I had imagined. We talked a bit about the situation, but soon moved on when she asked me how my mom was—the heartbreak part of our visit.

My mom's brain had been hijacked by dementia, and, well, I could write a whole lot about what it feels like to watch someone you love being devoured by this condition. But, mostly, witnessing the rapid cognitive and life changes of our matriarch—my mom—caused a sense of darkness and dread to descend upon me and my family at a rate that left us all feeling like someone had dimmed the light in our lives.

Lisa looked at me tenderly. "Maybe that's it," she said. "Maybe you need to receive light right now instead of sharing it."

I sat back in my chair, stared at her for a moment, and then tears began to stream down my face.

A Light in the Darkness

Sometimes when we're going through a difficult time or grieving, we find support in our friends or relatives. Even though we might only see them once or twice a year, and maybe only for a very short visit, their love for us is powerful. In our times of darkness, they're thinking of us, praying for us, holding us up. They're sending light our way; so when we're ready, we can let in that light. Maybe the darkness has been with us for a day, maybe a week, maybe months, or a year or more, but now we can let that light in and allow the pulse, the energy, the power of that light to replenish us, to help us heal.

If you're in a time of darkness, please take a moment to close your eyes and let in all the love and care and light people are sending you. Let it in.

In the darkness, we find our light.

And if you're not in a time of darkness, please also close your eyes and think of the humans in your life—or the people you've only read about or only seen or heard about on social media or the news—those humans who need love, prayers, and light. Send them some of your light.

Our light is reciprocal. We share our light knowing it will always come back to us. Maybe not from the same person we share it with, perhaps not even the same week or month, but that light will always come back. This I know for sure.

I also know that we are in a reciprocal relationship with that light, and part of our work in this life is to make sure that Mother Earth is in a reciprocal relationship with our light. Just as we get light from her—from the plants, the trees, the sparkles on water—we must also give light back. That way, we care for her—our mother, the Earth. We are stewards and caretakers of the land we live on. We nourish the land, we keep the water and air clean. We do our work to be caretakers of Mother Earth, to give her light so that perhaps she will find her way back to thriving again. If enough of us give her light, I truly believe she will thrive again. And then, so will we.

The Whir of a Hummingbird

After my visit with Lisa, I crawled into bed and expressed my gratitude for the day's gifts. I also asked that I wake up with clarity on my next step forward with my big idea.

I woke up with the clear message: *Cancel the series.* Over the next couple of days, I connected with the four beautiful humans who had agreed to be my guests. Interestingly, as I shared my vulnerability and truth, so did they. They were in similar places in their lives where replenishing their own light was the priority.

But the idea just kept buzzing around in my head. Not like a mosquito, because they are annoying, but more like the whir of a hummingbird. I kept thinking about the people who helped me in dark times—those who shared their light so I could navigate through the darkness. Sometimes, even a little bit of light to illuminate a way forward can make a world of difference! So I turned to something that always gives me light—writing and sharing stories.

When I first submitted this manuscript to my publisher in early 2024, the dementia that had found its way to my mom's brain was causing much anguish for me and everyone who loved her. A couple of months later, after a fall and a short hospital stay, my dear mom died in the early morning of June 8, 2024.

At the same time, a thirty-five-year friendship came to an end. We don't talk often enough about the difficulty of choosing to bring closure to a friendship. Some days, the grief over losing that friendship weighs heavily on my chest like a suitcase full of our memories—our laughter, adventures, secrets, and sisterhood. The weight I am trying to make bearable is the knowledge that no new memories will be added to that suitcase.

And as if those two losses weren't enough,

a couple of months later, my wife was diagnosed with cancer: stage 3 melanoma and lymphoma. All these experiences that had previously been in my mental filing cabinet under *Unimaginable* had now become imaginable and real.

It's hard to believe all of that happened in just four months. Sometimes, I wonder how I'm still standing. And then I remember: every single day, I have had to consciously foster my own light and be open to receiving light.

And through it all, I have learned that light and love can come from the most unexpected people and places.

The Five Ways of Being

Woven throughout this book are short stories, thoughts, reflections, and questions. Some pages have only a sentence or two to ponder. You can read this book from start to finish, or you can open it to a page and let the message there be your guide for the day. Or perhaps you will find the answer to a question you have been asking yourself or a decision you have been grappling with. The reflection questions are meant for just that—something to think about in the quiet parts of your day, and if you don't have any quiet parts, maybe that is the first question to ask yourself: How do I create some space for quiet moments in my life? Even ten minutes can nourish our spirits and add to our light. The reflection questions can also be conversation starters with friends and family. And the stories, well, stories help us understand ourselves, each other, and the world around us. They help us understand the past and inspire possibilities for the future. They are a form of medicine, and I hope the stories in this book help you remember stories in your life.

Throughout, I emphasize the importance of thanksgiving. I don't mean the holiday that is celebrated in the fall, but rather a worldview. A worldview that holds giving thanks at every opportunity as vital to our existence, and a worldview that reminds us that all good things begin with gratitude. Thanksgiving also reminds me that I am in a reciprocal relationship with gratitude. I offer thanks for the giving of what is to come.

In the dark times in life, gratitude can be a difficult place to start. Perhaps it feels like there's very little to be grateful for. If this is where you are right now, I invite you to start here: Before you get out of bed in the morning, offer thanks for your safe passage through the night and the gift of another day. And then, when you feel ready to deepen your gratitude, offer thanks for three elements of your life for which you are grateful.

Each chapter focuses on one of five ways of being: gratitude, love, joy, happiness, and hope. Some might call these disciplines or principles, but I associate both of those words with rules, and I'm not a huge fan of rules. Instead, I think of these as ways of being or practices. When we cultivate these ways of being, focus on them, seek them out, create them, and share them, they nourish our spirits and foster light within us—light that we can then share with each other and, in many ways, with all living beings.

Gratitude opens the doors for goodness and grace.

Love is medicine.

Joy is in the seemingly small, day-to-day moments in life.

Happiness is when you feel your heart open, and light weaves its way in and back out and then back in again.

Hope is believing the future will be better than today, and having the self-determination to make it so.

I often get asked, "What is the difference between joy and happiness?" This is a fantastic question and one that is really quite personal. What brings me joy might bring someone else a feeling of happiness, and vice versa. I think the easiest way for me to differentiate between the two is by sharing a story.

It had been a long February. The days were still short, and we'd had a month of rain—no sun at all. Plus, my wife was recovering from three major surgeries to remove cancer. It had been work to generate light!

One day we received an invitation to go to the movies with our little nephew, Luca. It was going to be his first time.

I absolutely love going to the movies! There is something magical about settling in with a bag of popcorn and being transported into a story. I find it inspiring to watch what was once a spark of an idea in someone's imagination become a full-fledged work of creativity. It's one of my favourite things to do and always leaves me feeling happier. Yes, some days feelings of happiness are absent, but it is during those times that I have learned that happiness is not a destination. Instead, it is about generating or noticing experiences that help me feel *happier*.

This invitation to the movie theatre was just the medicine I needed. The big chairs and the treats enthralled Luca, but when the screen lit up for the first time and the trailers began, his eyes doubled in size. His hand, full of popcorn, stopped midway to his mouth, which fell open in awe, and his toes pointed straight forward.

Joy!

He looked at his parents and then at us, his aunties, and we all mirrored his joy back to him. He giggled and then turned back to the screen. Joy remained present for a few minutes longer, and then he settled deeper into his chair and became engrossed in Paddington's adventure.

While joy came in moments that afternoon at the movies, the feeling of happiness lasted the rest of the day.

Reflection

How do *you* differentiate joy and happiness?

The Light Always Returns

The five ways of being—gratitude, love, joy, happiness, and hope—fill us with light and provide us with the energy and capacity to share our light with the world around us. For me, the self-determination that supports hope amounts to who and how I can be in the world. It is having the ability to design my life as I want it to be, not as others want me to be or live, but rather, what brings light to my heart. Self-determination is my way of sharing the bundle of gifts I've been blessed with, my way of contributing and caring for the world. Ultimately, it is the light that flickers in my heart and eyes.

And, yes, there are days, sometimes weeks or months, when the flicker is barely there, but it remains steadfast. It is in these times that practising the five ways of being is essential. My "work" in this life is to pursue and experience these emotions as much as possible; to determine what I will pay attention to and what, where, and with whom I will share my time and energy; and to have faith and inner knowing that the flicker will get stronger again.

And when I say "who," I mean the humans in our lives, but I also mean all living beings. For example, walking in the forest and leaning against a tree for a few moments can change our brain chemistry. Sitting by a creek with our heart on the downstream side can help us to let go; whereas, if we sit with our heart on the upstream side, whatever we want to let go of will return to us. Watching a squirrel collect nuts for the winter can remind us to plan and prepare. Sometimes this means preparing for the actual winter season, and sometimes it means preparing for a winter of our heart.

Our light is like the cycle of the moon. Sometimes we feel dynamic, bright, energized, and full. It takes no effort to shine and be a light for our journey and for others. Other times, we feel like the tiny crescent of a new moon, barely lit up and with little, if any, light to share. This is when we need others to share their light with us. Between these times, every stage moves from fullness and being a light to finding your light dissipating and moving toward the crescent. The beauty of it is that every crescent moon will once again become full. Not overnight, but in due time.

Perhaps like you, I have had some extremely long crescent moon phases in my life. Times when I wondered if I would ever feel full again.

And yet, the light always returns.

Gratitude shares light with love.

Love shares light with joy.

Joy shares light with happiness.

Happiness shares light with hope.

Hope shares light with gratitude.

And the circle continues.

And the light reverberates.

One

Gratitude

Gratitude opens the doors for goodness and grace.

All good things begin
with gratitude.

Guidance from Our Ancestors

On my desk, I have a small white frame, and on the pink paper inside are these words:

Yes

Not Yet

We have something even better in mind for you

These three responses are my guidance, my touchstone. When I ask for something or want something to occur, usually something that I think would be pretty cool or is important to me, these three responses help me remember that I am being guided and cared for by my Ancestors. They help me navigate the world and share my gifts in the best way possible. They can help each and every one of us.

Sure, there are times when I still feel disappointed if something doesn't work out, but when I look at these three responses, the disappointment passes more quickly. Instead, I move into curiosity. I wonder what is going to unfold. How will I be called on and used in a good way? How is that time going to be needed differently?

Everything changes when I shift to those perspectives, especially how I feel. Gratitude always emerges because I know, in my deepest core, that my Ancestors are always taking care of me, and they always will. Not always as I imagine or expect, but exactly how I need in order to foster my continued growth and protection.

Be grateful for adversity.

Go where you are appreciated,
not where you are tolerated.

Rejection Is Protection

I was checking my emails on my lunch break while facilitating a workshop in northern British Columbia, and a message upset me. Ironically, I don't remember what it was, but I remember that I had not gotten something I wanted. A writing grant? A facilitation opportunity? A contract?

Whatever it was, I was pretty disappointed, so I called my friend Richard Van Camp. He listened to me in his usual gentle way, and then simply said, "Sometimes, rejection is protection."

I felt the truth of that to my core. And I knew, without a shadow of a doubt, that it was true in this situation, and has been true in many situations in my life!

When I have a few moments to reflect—and let my ego get out of the way—this profound statement, "Rejection is protection," almost always takes the sting out of a disappointment. I am comforted by the reminder that my Ancestors are taking good care of me and protecting me.

Reflection

Take a moment to reflect on a time when you really wanted something to happen and it didn't.

Do you now see how you were being protected and taken care of?

What We Focus on Multiplies

When you wake up in the morning, before your feet touch the floor, and definitely before you reach for your phone, I invite you to offer thanks for a safe passage through the night. And then, offer thanks for three aspects of your life for which you are grateful.

At bedtime, offer gratitude for your safe passage through the day, and offer thanks for three aspects of your day for which you are grateful.

Give thanks for the safe passage through the night, and the gift of living another day.

Reflection

Do this every day for a few weeks and notice how you feel.

Do this for a few months and notice the difference in your relationships.

Do this every day for a year and notice the changes in your life.

Focus On Blessings to Foster a Grateful Heart

One of my fondest childhood memories is of my mom tucking me into bed and asking me, "What was the best part of your day?"

This was a beautiful way for her to prompt me to reflect on the day. It ultimately began a reflection practice that helped me focus on the blessings and highlights of my day. I always found that on those nights, I slept better and woke up the next day with a lightness in my heart and spirit.

When my wife, Rhonda, and I had our children, this reflection question became part of their bedtime routine. It was a way to connect. A tender, gentle, and grateful way to bring closure to the day. I was always curious about what our children would share. These moments provided glimpses into what cultivated happiness and joy in their day so that, as a parent, I could understand more of what brought light into their hearts and lives.

Reflection

What was the best part
of your day?

Offer gratitude for the "teachers" who come throughout our lives. The ones who help us learn, grow, evolve, and love.

Take a moment to think about all the people who have shared their light with you, who have loved you into being.

Go visit them.

Call them, send them a note in the mail, email, FaceTime, or text.

Share your gratitude for their light, for their presence in your life.

Be prepared for
beautiful surprises!

Cultivate the vibration of gratitude.

Angels Among Us

My last semester of nursing school was a practicum back in my hometown of Kamloops, BC. During that time, I'd often visit my dear friend and former college roommate Kelly at the restaurant where she worked the evening shift. We decided that when the semester ended and I'd graduated from nursing school, we would go on a trip abroad. Neither of us had ever travelled. Sure, both of us had camped, but we didn't come from families who took tropical holidays in the winter, and we didn't go away on summer vacation—unless you count driving twenty-four hours in a cigarette-smoke-filled car to visit family in Saskatchewan. Planning a trip to another country was a big deal!

Our initial plan was to go to Brazil, but the travel agent in Vancouver said he would not sell us tickets. Apparently, he thought it was too dangerous for two young women who spoke no Portuguese and "looked like us" to travel alone in Brazil in 1990.

We were back at square one, deciding where to go. One night, when I was visiting Kelly after work, a high school friend, Bill, who also worked at the restaurant, joined us. "Last year, I went to the Dominican Republic and had a blast," he said. "I'd highly recommend. Beaches are amazing, food is good, and the beer is cheap. Like crazy cheap."

I was sold with the mention of cheap beer, but I hadn't even heard of the Dominican Republic. My face must've shown my ignorance because Bill explained that it was a country in the Caribbean on the same island as Haiti. To be honest, that information didn't really help me much.

As Kelly and I were getting ready to leave the restaurant, Bill added, "If you decide to go and you're along the Malecon in Puerto Plata and you happen to meet a guy named Isidro Comacho, say hi to him for me. He'll remember me as Blue Jays Bill."

When I got home, I grabbed the *D* volume of the encyclopedia—these were the days before Google—and looked up the Dominican Republic. I was intrigued. I noticed it was close to Grand Cayman, where my friend Janet was living and teaching scuba diving. I made a few notes in my travel journal, including Bill's comment about Isidro, and Kelly and I began to plan our trip.

On the day we were leaving, my mom dropped me off at Kelly's. I was expecting her to stop the truck, get out, and hug me, and then I'd be on my way. But no, my mom slowed to a rolling pace, reached across me, opened the door, and gave me a little push. "There you go," she said. "Be safe and have fun."

I looked at her. I don't know what kind of special goodbye I expected, but it certainly wasn't this.

She gave me another little push and a nod of her head. I got out, grabbed my pack from the pickup bed, and watched her drive off.

As a parent now, I understand how incredibly difficult that must have been for her. Kelly and I were going to a country that almost no one we knew had heard of, and no one in my family had ever travelled like this. My mom had no reference that it would all be okay. And it was 1990—no cellphones, no internet, only handwritten letters and the odd phone call from the telephone centres in big cities. But thank goodness! Because had she known what was about to unfold, well—yikes!

Our trip began in Grand Cayman, and it was an absolutely extraordinary time! It all started when we got off the plane and I felt my first burst of tropical heat. I instantly knew I wanted to feel that as many times in my life as possible. We slept on Janet's covered deck, and she introduced us to white sand beaches, turquoise waters, and snorkelling. I had no idea there was a whole other magnificent world right there under the water. And then there was how cold beer tasted after a day in the sun and sea. I felt a sense of freedom, joy, and vitality that was just as new to me as all the experiences I was having.

After three weeks in Grand Cayman, we flew to the Dominican Republic. The only Spanish we spoke was *baño* and *cerveza*, but "bathroom" and "beer" would not get us far. Once we got through customs, we were bombarded by numerous men in orange overalls yelling in Spanish that they could help us with our luggage, get us a taxi, or find us a place to stay. We managed to navigate through them and get out of the airport and into a taxi. Thank goodness I had written the hotel name on a piece of paper because the taxi driver spoke no English, and we spoke no Spanish. Thinking back now, I am embarrassed at how disrespectful it was of us to travel to a Spanish-speaking country without taking the time to learn even a bit of the language.

As the taxi took off, I realized part of the floor was missing like the cars in *The Flintstones*. I had to be careful where I put my feet! I tried to match Kelly's excitement, but inside I was thinking, *Oh my god.* WTF *have we done?*

From Stranger to Saviour

The next morning we went to the front desk, where we were grateful to find English-speaking staff who helped us figure out how to change our money. We needed to go to the Malecon and walk down the boardwalk to the bank. After only about ten steps, a young man approached us. He was friendly and spoke enough English for us to have a conversation. I could tell that Kelly had the same good feeling about him as I did.

His name was Isidro.

But in the flurry of new experiences, his name didn't resonate with me. He took us to change our money on the black market, which we didn't know at the time was illegal. Even as I write this, I think about how naive we were and can't help but shake my head.

For a couple of weeks, he took care of us. He helped with anything we needed—finding a place to live, taking us to local food markets. We spent a lot of time with him and his buddy Alejandro and started learning Spanish. One day, we were at a bar, and I overheard him introduce himself to someone as Isidro Comacho.

I heard his last name and wondered why it sounded so familiar.

When we got back to where we were living, I opened my journal and, sure enough, there it was: "If you decide to go and you're along the Malecon in Puerto Plata and you happen to meet a guy named Isidro Comacho, say hi to him for me. He'll remember me as Blue Jays Bill."

I showed it to Kelly. We had no words, just a mixture of shock, awe, and gratitude. The next day, I showed my journal entry to Isidro. He had a minor flip-out. Of course, he remembered Blue Jays Bill!

What stands out most for me is how well Isidro took care of us—he saved us in many ways, including when we were being robbed at gunpoint. Isidro took us to Santo Domingo to stay with his family and experience his community and culture. When our Spanish was strong enough, he helped us figure out where to travel safely in his beautiful country.

I truly believe he was an angel. An angel who crossed our path and shared his light to help us survive. I am not sure we would have made it through our time in the Dominican Republic without the care, guidance, and support of Isidro Comacho. I will always be grateful for him.

Reflection

Who are the angels who have crossed your path and helped you in times of need?

Give thanks for
beautiful surprises.

The words you speak
weave the life you live.

Speak words of gratitude,
thanksgiving, and appreciation.

Speak words of hope,
possibilities, and miracles.

Speak words of kindness,
love, and joy.

The words you speak
weave the life you live.

Our thoughts create our emotions, and our emotions create our thoughts.

This cycle is why it's vital that we pay attention to and foster thoughts that generate the feelings of love, joy, happiness, and hope.

On those days when love, joy, happiness, or hope seem out of reach or even impossible, start with gratitude.

What would GRATITUDE do?

Gratitude shines light on gratitude.

Gratitude shines light on gratitude.

Gratitude shines light on gratitude.

Gratitude shines light on love.

Two

Love

Love is medicine.

Let love light the way.

Cookie People

This is one of my favourite terms of endearment—cookie people. My first cookie person was Mrs. Gladish. When I was five, we lived in Rutland, BC; she was our next-door neighbour. Somehow, she always knew when it was a tough day in our house, and she'd come through the back gate with a plate full of cookies still warm from the oven. She would sit at the kitchen table and visit with us as we had a cookie or two, and with each bite, I felt better. Sure, the cookies were delicious, but Mrs. Gladish was the medicine that changed my heart. And not only mine—she would change the whole energy in our house.

Cookie people can come into our lives for a moment and change our trajectory, or they can travel with us for a long period of time along our life's journey. They are people who see something in us that others haven't seen before, or maybe they have a unique relationship with us that inspires us. They see the gifts we have been blessed with and support us in cultivating them. Maybe they speak our future—like the woman at the University of Victoria who, after my interview for the School of Social Work, said to me, "I look forward to reading your book one day." It took twenty years for me to write that book, but she was one of the first people who saw my gift and spoke my future for me. She was the first pebble of possibility.

One of my cookie people was my auntie Ellen. She was an incredibly special human being—not just for me, but for many people. I learned so much from her, and her influence on my life played a big part in making me who I am today.

One icy February night in Kamloops, she picked me up from my indoor softball practice. On our way home, we drove past Schoening's funeral home. The sign read minus twenty-eight degrees Celsius—the kind of cold that makes your nose hairs freeze and your face tingle. A bit farther down the road, we drove past a woman who appeared to be unhoused. She was pushing a cart and was not dressed for the weather—wearing runners, a light jacket, and no toque or gloves.

Auntie Ellen said, "Oh, there's Bonnie," and pulled over. Then she turned to me and said, "Give me your winter jacket and gloves."

I was raised in a single-parent household, so my winter jacket was a valuable commodity. But I was also raised to know that when your auntie asks you to do something, you do it! I took off my winter jacket and gloves, and my auntie took off her boots and toque. She reached into her wallet for twenty dollars and got out of the car. I watched as she spoke with Bonnie and then dressed her in our clothes. She tucked the twenty-dollar bill into the jacket's inside pocket, kissed Bonnie on the cheek, got back in the car, and drove me home. She never said anything about it.

I didn't have the words to describe it then, but it was one of the most beautiful acts of humanity I ever witnessed. My auntie was working as a psychiatric nurse at that time. She worked in the community with the unhoused population and those struggling with addictions and mental health. To say Bonnie was one of her clients is a very Western way to characterize their relationship. To my auntie, Bonnie was a community member, someone to care for and love. From my auntie,

I learned the importance of community, holding up people's dignity, and treating people as human beings, not clients or numbers.

After a year in college, I applied to psychiatric nursing school, because I was inspired by one of my cookie people: my auntie Ellen.

You Are a Cookie Person Too

Remember, you are also a cookie person—maybe to one person or maybe to many. This is part of what it means to be in reciprocal relationships. Cookie people come into our lives to help us through difficult times, inspire us to believe in ourselves, and help us be bigger than we think we can be. They see our gifts and support us in going after our dreams. In return, we do the same for others.

Reflection

I invite you to reach out to your cookie people—or better yet, visit them. Spend time really connecting—share the importance of their contributions to your journey and to the human you are. If they have passed over to the other side, you can still connect with them. You can write them a letter and either keep it or burn it. You can go for a quiet walk in nature and talk to them in your head. You can go to a religious or spiritual place, say prayers, and light a candle for them.

Love is Medicine

Trust in the joy.

Trust in the bounty.

Trust in the beauty.

Trust in the glory.

Trust in the unfolding.

And remember that

you are here to experience.

Love is Medicine

Every act of kindness is an act of prayer and light and love.

In one of my all-time favourite songs, Tina Turner sings, "What's love got to do with it?"

My answer—EVERYTHING!

How Do We Carry What We Cannot Bear?

Kelly and I went to high school together and were college roommates. We had just come back from travelling together when she found me in the fetal position on the bathroom floor, a pool of tears cradling my cheek. Slowly, she lifted me to a sitting position, wrapped her arms around me, and rested her head against mine.

Eventually, Kelly broke the silence. "Monique, I'm worried about you. I love you very much, but you need help. Your drinking is out of control—you're out of control." Her tone conveyed love and care, as well as fear.

When I finally got the courage to look at her, I was shocked. There was no judgment in her eyes—none at all—just love—the opposite of what I felt for myself.

I wanted to agree with her, to tell her that my drinking—and I—was out of control. But I knew if I said those words, I would never be able to take them back. They'd be out there forever. There'd be no going back to my safe ride on the denial bus. Even if I kept drinking, nothing would be the same, because I knew that I needed help. Deep in my heart was the truth—if I kept drinking, my path would lead to an early death. Either my drinking would kill me, or I would take my own life. The pain was just too much.

"I need help," I heard myself whisper. "I need help." And then I collapsed, sobbing, in her arms.

After I released a burden of tears and anguish, Kelly helped me up off the bathroom floor and moved me to a comfortable chair in the living room. She made us mint tea and called her mom's friend Bob, who was sober and had been involved with Alcoholics Anonymous (AA) for many years. He came over that night and sat with us for hours. He offered to take me to an AA meeting, but I wasn't ready for that level of acknowledgement of my addiction. Geez, I was only twenty-two.

Although I continued to drink for a few more months, the seed of sobriety had been planted. My favourite beer didn't taste as good, the buzz was harder to reach, and my hangovers grew more vicious.

Even though I wasn't fully aware of it at a conscious level, my journey toward sobriety and a new life had begun. Many times during my initial recovery, there were opportunities to go back out. The minutes, hours, and days ahead required more strength and resilience than I could ever imagine I had.

Rooted in Recovery

On April 26, 1991, I officially began my sobriety journey. I started attending AA meetings regularly and was grateful to have sponsors like Charlotte Manuel and Opie Oppenheim, from whom I learned so much!

It wasn't easy being a young woman in AA. At my first meeting, one of the so-called old-timers looked at me and said, "I've probably spilled more than you've drank."

I also began sessions with David Antoine, a counsellor at the Kamloops Friendship Centre. In August 1992, after much encouragement from David, I went to Round Lake Treatment Centre. There, everything changed for me. Yes, the counselling helped tremendously, but the impact of culture and ceremony was even more profound.

Throughout my almost thirty-five years of recovery, there have been plenty of times when I wasn't sure if I could bear what was unfolding in my life. Before my time at Round Lake, I was like a piece of sagebrush—tossed around by the slightest breeze. But during treatment, I put roots down in the ground. Now, when the winds of life blow hard, I bend, but I no longer get tossed around. My roots—my culture, family, and connection to the land—keep me grounded, keep me rooted.

Reflection

What helps keep *you* grounded and rooted?

Loving is a practice of an awake mind, an open heart, and a grateful spirit.

Loving the earth and all living beings is a practice of love, and it requires that we also love ourselves.

Love is our true intelligence.

Fill a Room with Love

During her visits, Grandma Tilly taught me about being generous, telling the truth and always treating other people with dignity and respect. Every night after dinner, she and I would sit outside, and she would pull out her pipe bag and load her pipe for her evening smoke. "C'mere, li'l Tilly, gather under my wing and let's talk about the day." With me tucked up close to her, we'd review our escapades. She'd ask me, "What'd you learn today? What was the best part?"

I missed her so much once she'd gone home, but Grandma Tilly made a point of staying in touch by phone. She was on a party line in her community, and it was common to be on a call with her and have someone cut in.

"Who's on the line?" the person would ask.

"It's Tilly. I'm on with li'l Tilly, an' we gonna be a while."

Once when I called her to talk about some things I was upset about at school she told me, "What you gotta remember, Tilly, is that everyone's born with love in their hearts. Sometimes life takes that away, but we all born with it. So, whenever you enter a room, in your imagination, fill it with love. And make enough room for everyone else to fill that room with love, too. That, my girl, is when good things happen."

I always felt better after my talks with Grandma Tilly. Her teachings, words, and sayings were like medicine to me.

Reflection

In what ways do you fill
a room with love?

You can love someone and
say goodbye to them and
still miss them.

Every.

Single.

Day.

Part of our journey is
transforming the cards we've
been dealt so the next generation
has less to heal from.

More room

to cultivate

their dreams

and gifts.

Letter from Love

Dear Love, what would you have me know today?

Stay Home! And we know you think this means your house, but what we mean is to stay in the home of your heart. Cultivate this home, nurture this home and tend to this home like you tend to your garden. We, love, and our sister, joy, are always in this home of your heart.

We want you to know you are safe to be seen. You are blanketed with guidance and protection. Please, go out in the world and share the gifts you have been blessed with AND enjoy the blessings we send to you in reciprocity for sharing your gifts.

Remember, everyone has a story, and we never truly know what that story is or how it might be impacting them when your paths cross. Bring light, bring care and bring gentleness, and bring us LOVE. And please, bring these gifts to yourself as well. Your judgements of yourself do not reflect the beauty in your heart and spirit.

Remember the teaching that Love is Medicine. Wrap yourself in a blanket of love—let our warmth be your medicine for this moment, this hour, this day … for always. And pay attention to our sister, the emotion and feeling of joy. These aren't always the big moments. Joy is your first sip of coffee in the morning after the foam has settled just right, when your family lingers at the dinner table long after the meal has been eaten, when your mom tells you to "have fun," when the gentle smoke of your sweetgrass braid wakes up every cell and you can't help but inhale deeper so the memories and strength of your Ancestors wake up too, when you walk in the forest, when your cat curls up on your chest and purrs, and when you are barefoot working in the yard and garden.

These are the moments to pay attention to—these are the moments when we are both present—love and joy. These are the moments that both fuel you to go out into the world and keep your heart home full. And in the dark times, which do come, call on us, love. We will always return. Actually, we never leave; sometimes it's just hard for you to experience us, but love is always here.

Reflection

I encourage you to visit Elizabeth Gilbert's *Letters from Love* on Substack.

Perhaps you will be inspired to start writing your own Letters from Love.

Love, where would you
have me go?

Love, what would you
have me do?

Love, what would you
have me share?

Love, who would you
have me meet?

Love, what would you
have me say?

Love, how would you
have me respond?

Love, what would you
have me cultivate?

Love, how would you
have me share my gifts?

Love, what would you
have me learn?

Let

Others

Voluntarily

Evolve

Be Open

For the first ten years of my parents' separation, they could hardly stand to be in the same room. Then, when their first grandchildren, our twins, were born, something softened in both of them. It felt like they realized that the magic they had created had now extended to another generation. It was a bond they would never have with any other human.

Then, when my sister got married, the softening increased. I even saw them laugh together. It felt like a miracle. Like the eggshells we had been walking on for almost two decades had hardened and become a pathway. Like maybe, just maybe, we could find a way back to feeling like a family again. Don't get me wrong, I had no illusions that they would get back together. Too much had happened. There were too many hurts and too many betrayals to come back from.

Jump ahead another five years, and my niece Brianna was born. The whole family decided to spend Christmas together in Kamloops at my sister's house, where my mom and her partner lived across the street. Yes, there were very weird times that Christmas! All of us together—AWKWARD! But we did it, and we did it without any drama or trauma. During that holiday, there were moments when it was just my parents doing dishes or visiting at the kitchen table. A bit of a friendship was being forged. It is amazing how babies and children can bring a family together.

Fast-forward a few years, and my dad's marriage ended. He moved to live with my sister and her family. This move meant that whenever my mom came over to visit my sister, my dad would come up from his suite and join in.

One time, I was visiting and my sister and her husband were building a new house. She wanted us to see the progress, so we all piled into the car—my sister, our parents, and me. It was the first time we had been alone together in at least thirty years. I had to open my window slightly, as the bounty of emotions and energy swirling in that car was so intense. Not in a bad way, but I wondered what my life would have been like had our family stayed together.

There was a sacredness to those couple of hours the four of us spent alone together—a sacredness that was a salve to the wounds each of us carried, a sacredness that opened the path for a new way for us to come together and be a family. It was like my sister taking us to see the foundation of the house they were building helped our family return to our original foundation and redesign how we wanted to be together as a family.

A Steadfast Love

Over the years, my parents spent more and more time together and developed a companionship that comes from knowing someone for over fifty-five years. And when my dad died in 2021, we all felt the loss, including my mom. As he requested, we laid his ashes to rest on top of a mountain with a magnificent view overlooking a lake he loved.

In the years that followed, my sister and I had the difficult conversations with my mom about where she wanted to be laid to rest. Not difficult in the conflict kind of way, but rather, these conversations between a parent and adult child are tender, surreal, and, for me, they were heart-wrenching. I could not imagine my life without my mom in it. I always felt a part of me dissociate from myself during those conversations. But as they unfolded, and in her moments of deepest clarity, my mom let us know she wanted to be laid to rest beside my dad on top of the mountain.

Their love remained steadfast even after decades of hurt, heartache, and disappointment. I often find myself thinking about their love story. I sometimes wonder if they'd had different communication tools, less financial pressure, more support, if life had even been a tad bit gentler, might they have been able to make it? I will never know, but I do know, in time, they made it back to each other in their own way.

I think of them up there on that mountain, side by side, with their beautiful view, and I believe there is peace and joy in their hearts.

Breathe in the stars'
celestial wisdom.

And let it pulse through
your body and merge with
your ancestral wisdom.

This sacred combination is the
expression of our gifts.

Of how we contribute to the
wellness of the world.

The expression of our gifts is
always rooted in love.

What would LOVE do?

Love shines light on love.

Love shines light on love.

Love shines light on love.

Love shines light on joy.

Three

Joy

Joy is in the seemingly small, day-to-day moments in life.

Step into the channel of joy.

And invite others to join you.

Discovering Joy

When I think back to my childhood, my family—yes, my parents, but also my aunties and uncles—taught me to seek, experience, and pay attention to moments of joy. I felt both happiness and joy when we were out on the land. Happiness was gathering wood for the winter, picking berries, fishing, and roasting marshmallows over the fire. Joy was when the last of the firewood was loaded in the truck, when I discovered a berry patch ripe for picking, when a fish bit and my rod snapped forward and I reeled in as hard as I could, and when I toasted a marshmallow to golden-brown perfection. Joy was everyone loading into the car for a Sunday drive to collect bottles from the side of the road. Joy was when my mom had her curling team over and I'd hear her laugh, like really laugh. Playing sports also brought me joy—playing road hockey with the boys across the street and pretending I was Guy Lafleur; this was the mid-1970s, and there weren't any female hockey players to emulate yet. Later, in my teens, I often felt joy when I caught a fly ball or scored a goal on the field hockey pitch.

From my mom, I learned about the importance of creating joy in difficult times. One specific time really stands out. We had just moved to Nelson, BC, where, unbeknownst to my mom, my dad had not yet secured a house for us, nor did he have the means to do so. We were camping at the beach. I was ten and my sister was seven, so a summer at the beach was kind of fun. My sister and mom slept in the camper, and I was initially excited to sleep with my dad in the tent, but the novelty of sleeping on the ground wore off after a couple of nights. As did the appeal of the communal shower and toilets.

This ordeal caused my mom visible distress. We had moved from our beautiful home in Kelowna and were now homeless. She was isolated and had no way to develop friendships or community. Each day, her anguish became more and more apparent. She only came out of the camper to have a cigarette and eventually stopped making dinner—instead, handing us the pack of wieners and bag of hot dog buns. She downright refused to talk to my dad or even look at him. In hindsight, I understand how devastating it was for her to move from the house she loved, her garden, her friends, her curling club, her job, her sense of community and belonging, only to arrive in Nelson to discover we had no home. Well, it was almost too much for her to bear.

When I reflect on that time, I am in awe of her ability to ensure my sister and I still had moments of joy in the midst of her darkness. I think seeing our joy also brought her joy—or at least I hope it did!

I know this might sound odd, but laundry day was an occasion for joy. We'd load our laundry into bags and, with them slung over our shoulders, we'd trudge across the iconic Big Orange Bridge to the laundromat. Thank goodness it was summer and most of our clothes were light because those bags were heavy! The first wave of joy came with our arrival in the air-conditioned laundromat. The next wave was the sensation of the cool metal of the chair on my back and thighs. My mom always rested for a few moments before springing out of her chair to announce, "C'mon, girls, the laundry isn't going to do itself!" Once the clothes were in the wash, my sister and I would embark on our next quest for joy.

In the 1980s and '90s, many of the washers had a spinner in the middle. If you unscrewed the top of the spinner, you could lift the whole piece at the bottom, and find all kinds of goodies—mostly coins that had fallen out of people's pockets, and sometimes jewellery. The jewellery we'd turn in, but the coins we kept. When the laundry was done and our bags were packed with neatly folded clothes, we'd walk next door to the Dairy Queen. Somehow, we always found enough money in the bottom of those dryers to buy us all ice cream. Yes, another wave of joy! And, sometimes, we'd even find enough to buy French fries too. I didn't have words for it then, but now I would say that what I felt was pure joy when I watched my mom's expression as she would dip a French fry into her ice cream.

I use the metaphor of joy coming in waves because the media in our society today tells us that joy should be like a tsunami that overwhelms us. But just like the waves that come into shore consistently as part of the ocean cycle, joy also consistently shows up as part of our life cycle. It's up to us to pay attention, notice the joy, and let that feeling in.

To experience the beauty and nourishment of joy.

To feel the hope that the light of joy gives us.

Reflection

What childhood memories do you have of joy?

Moments of joy keep us going.

"Even a wounded world
is feeding us.

Even a wounded world holds us,
giving us moments of wonder
and joy.

I choose joy over despair.

Not because I have my head in the sand, but because joy is what the Earth gives me daily and I must return the gift."

—Dr. Robin Wall Kimmerer

Chocolate Ice Cream

I have very few stories where I witnessed joy and my dad together; mostly, they involve driving his little twelve-foot aluminum boat, picking Saskatoon berries, and watching sports on TV, especially the Vancouver Canucks and Toronto Blue Jays. On his deathbed, he spoke of all his regrets, not his joys or happiness.

Even as I write this, I feel a stinging behind my eyes. I don't want to be disrespectful to the life my dad lived and the choices he made. He has been one of my greatest teachers. Being part of his life and living with the impact of his choices have been huge inspirations for how I consciously design my life, how I want to be in the world, and, especially, how I want to be in my relationships.

From September 2020 to January 2021, my sister, brother-in-law, and I, along with home support, cared for my dad at home as his cancer had spread to his bones and brain. In early January, we could no longer provide the advanced care he needed and had to make the excruciating decision to hospitalize him.

Even the best decision for everyone involved can still hurt like hell, both to make and to keep. This was one of those decisions.

All of this unfolded during the height of the COVID-19 pandemic, which meant that when he was transferred to hospice, we couldn't bring anything from home to make him feel more comfortable—no blankets, pillows, special coffee mug, flowers, or plants, not even photos. Nothing to make the experience of dying less sterile and more homey. There were no volunteers, no open kitchen for coffee, tea, or snacks, no sense of community or witnessing along this journey.

It wasn't how I'd heard others describe their hospice experiences. It was brutal!

Added to the stress, again because of the pandemic, only one person could visit my dad at a time. When you're visiting a loved one as they are preparing to die, either in hospice or at home, it can be so comforting to have another person there with you. It wasn't until the last two nights before his death that my sister and I were allowed to be with our dad together.

Grief is a difficult path to walk, especially when walking alone. Witnessing my dad deteriorate each day and suffer in pain was even more difficult for all of us because we had to do it alone.

But perhaps the most difficult part of the whole experience was listening to him share all his regrets from his life—the decisions he wished he hadn't made, the opportunities he didn't take, the days he spent working instead of fishing, and the family he left behind for what he thought was true love.

A Spoonful of Joy

I often think about three specific days in the six weeks before my dad died: the day the ambulance came to take him to the hospital, the family meeting with the hospital social worker and his care team where we shared with him that he was being transitioned to hospice instead of coming home, and the day I came to visit him at hospice and the nurse greeted me with, "Your dad thought he died last night."

I had stepped off the elevator and walked toward my dad's room when a nurse appeared by my side.

Before my startle response had settled, she told me, "Your dad thought he died last night." My nervous system spiked again, and my legs felt like they were going to buckle under me. Even though he was in hospice and I knew what was coming, her words caused the little girl in me to silently scream, *Nooooooo!* My heart pounded in my chest, my throat constricted, and my mouth was dry.

After she spoke to me for a couple more minutes, during which I honestly didn't hear a word she said, I made my way to his room. All I could see was the door handle, and even though I knew it was my hand reaching to open the door, I felt like I was watching a movie. The moaning from other patients echoed in my ears, and my stomach churned. I took a deep breath, exhaled slowly, and entered my dad's room.

He was asleep, as he was most of the time now. There is no crayon in the Crayola palette for the colour he had become. Even though I had seen my dad like this for a few weeks now, I was still taken aback. I took my usual position in a chair beside his bed and stared out the window, my imagination taking me far away from that room.

"I thought I died last night."

Those words startled me back to the present. I reached for my dad's hand, and he continued, "There was drumming. I walked toward the drumming. Auntie Ellen was there, Uncle Bert, and—" the sentence was cut off by a coughing attack. He grimaced in pain, and when he finally caught his breath, he went on, "There was a string attached to me, and it kept pulling me back. There was a bright light at the end of the string." He rested for a minute. "I always thought the light was supposed to be in front of you, not behind you, but I kept getting pulled back by the string."

"What was at the end of the string?" I asked. The little girl in me hoped he would say my sister and me and his grandchildren, that we were the light.

"Chocolate ice cream," he answered.

I giggled. I mean, really, what else could I do?

"Well, let's see if there's any chocolate ice cream in here." I checked the tiny fridge in his room, and even though he hadn't had food trays for a few days, one small serving of ice cream sat there on the shelf.

Chocolate. My dad's favourite.

I fed a little to him, and when he raised his hand, I knew he'd had enough. He rested for a while, then turned to me and said, "I could've done so much with my life." He looked at me for a moment, then his eyes slowly closed.

I watched his chest to make sure he was still breathing. He was. Initially, I heard the remorse in his words, "I could've done so much with my life," and felt deep sadness. But over time, after taking many walks in the forest and sharing this story with loved ones, I have developed compassion for him. I take his statement as a message to live my life to the fullest. To not find myself on my deathbed with regrets or wishes for different decisions or unfulfilled potential and dreams, but rather with a sense of peace, with reflections of a life where joy was part of the fabric that wove everything together.

Do I wish my sister and I had been at the end of my dad's string? For sure! But I also understand that he was grieving a life he wished he'd lived differently. As I fed him those spoonfuls of chocolate ice cream, I witnessed the joy it brought him, and that memory brings me joy.

My dad reminded me that joy comes from paying attention to the small pleasures in life.

In the darkness, a small joy can bring a lot of light.

And, yes, when I'm missing him, I have myself some chocolate ice cream.

Reflection

What small things do *you* do to feel joy?

Joy is little moments and details that remind our hearts and spirits that everything is going to be okay.

The moments that cause a smile to spread across our face.

The moments that cause our eyes to prickle with tears—not sad tears, but tears of joy and awe.

The moments that lift our hearts.

The moments when our lungs fill to capacity with air.

The moments that calm our nervous system.

Choose Joy

I went on a ten-day holiday and work trip with my wife, Rhonda, that started in New York City and ended in California. For years, New York City at Christmastime was on my bucket list for various reasons, but mostly for all the lights and displays the season brings. It was truly magical!

We had a long travel day from the East Coast to California, so I was grateful to see a coffee shop in the hotel lobby when we checked in that night. I had a big keynote address the next day and knew I'd need a li'l caffeinated support beforehand.

The next morning, I was up early and headed down to get some coffee. The line was long, but I could hear a joyful voice at the end of it. As the line moved and I got closer to my turn to order, I noticed a petite human working behind the counter. Yes, she was working, but she was also spreading joy. I started to hear her, "Good morning, love, what can I get you today?" Or "Good morning, what would help start your day in a happy way?"

I had a brief and lovely visit with her as I placed my order, after which I felt more energized as I headed across the lobby to tinker with my keynote—and I hadn't even had a sip of coffee yet! As I worked, I saw her treat each person with dignity and joy. I watched as people left the counter, changed. The heaviness, the agitation, the restlessness, the anxiousness that had been with them in the line was almost always replaced with a smile, a dropping of their shoulders, and a lightness to their steps.

The next morning, it was the same. I sat across the lobby and worked, but I was very aware of her voice and energy. It was such a gift to witness her sharing her joy and feel the energy of her joy reverberate throughout the lobby. She reminded me how much our energy can influence others and the space we are in.

A couple of days later, as Rhonda and I were waiting for the airport shuttle, there was no line at the coffee shop, so I went over and introduced myself. I learned her name was Maricela and she started work at five a.m., which meant she started her day every morning at four. I shared what I had noticed about her joy—how I felt energized by my interactions with her and her genuine care for those she served. She blushed and said how sweet that was to hear. I then asked her how she brought joy each morning.

She smiled and cocked her head. "No one's ever asked me that before. Hmmm, well, I guess it's this simple. Every morning you wake up and you have a decision to make—joy or no joy." She shrugged her shoulders. "It's that simple—I choose joy." Her sparkling dark eyes held my gaze for a moment, and then she continued, "And when someone gives me a kind word, or I turn a grumpy person into a happy or grateful one, or if they say, 'You made my day,' that fills up my joy, and then I have more joy to share. That's how joy works."

A smile came over my whole body. I thanked Maricela for the beautiful reminder to not only choose joy but to share joy.

Reflection

In what ways do *you* choose and share joy?

Let's light each other up!

Joy is powerful.

Not power over, but power
from within.

Joy is like the lightbulb that goes
on when we flick the switch
on the wall.

The power lights up the room.

Joy lights up the room.

Joy is powerful.

Lava Rocks

I remember coming home from my fourth twelve-hour graveyard shift on the Psych Unit at the hospital to find my mom placing a cookie sheet in the oven. But there weren't cookies on it. Instead, there were four lava rocks, each a bit bigger than a softball. Usually, these rocks were placed in the sacred fire for a Sweat Lodge ceremony, and once they were red hot, they were placed in the lodge. We know them as Grandfathers and Grandmothers.

I was a bit confused, both because of my utter exhaustion from my shifts and because of the peculiarity of seeing Grandfathers and Grandmothers sitting on top of the oven.

"What's going on here, Mom?" I asked.

"Uncle David gave them to me." She tilted her head to the lava rocks. "He said that when I need to have a sweat and can't get up to the lodge, I should put them in the oven until they're hot and then put them in an empty bathtub. To have my own ceremony by splashing water on them, saying my prayers, and cleansing."

Over the years, Mom held her own ceremony many times with those rocks in her tiny little bathroom. I noticed that, afterward, whatever was going on that inspired her need to nourish her spirit had been released and replaced by a glow of joy, lightheartedness, and serenity.

A Labour of Love

About six months after my mom died, my sister and I embarked on renovating our mom's house. It's weird, yes, legally my sister and I own the house, but somehow it will always be Mom's, or Kookum's, home.

Lois, a family friend close to my mom, was doing all the renovations. I couldn't imagine another person caring for my mom's house the same way. The work was a labour of love, and all along the way, miracles happened. Reminders and nudges from my mom that the veil between where she is "on the other side" and our lived reality is thin. For example, in every photo Lois sends of changes in what was Mom's bedroom, there is a ray of light streaming in. Some might try to explain this away because her bedroom is at the front of the house, but the photos were often taken when the sun was at the back of the house.

A couple of months into the renovations, my sister and I were driving when Lois called. "Kookum sure has been around lately," she informed us, and we both smiled. Of course, she had.

"How so?" I asked.

"Well, I always leave my tools in the same exact spot when I leave at the end of the day. I like to be organized. A few days ago, when I came in, my X-ACTO knife had moved to the kitchen counter. And then this morning when I came in, my tape measure was clear across the room, and it took me a while to find it." She giggled and added, "Good ol' Shirl is having fun playing tricks on me."

That was Mom! Lighthearted, playful, joyful.

Joy

When the darkness begins to
dissipate and the light finds her
way back in,

even for a moment,

there's a deep exhale.

A sweet relief.

Joy

A Message from Mom

The other day, my daughter Sadie popped in to visit Lois and see how the renovations were coming along. Over FaceTime, Sadie showed me all the beautiful changes in the house. When she got to the bathroom, Lois said, "I found the weirdest thing in here the other day."

Sadie looked at me on the screen and raised one eyebrow. We were both curious. Lots of "weird" things had occurred and been found since the renovations began.

Lois continued, "I was going to put the tiles in the next day, so I laid cardboard down in the tub to prevent any damage. The next morning, when I came in to start tiling—weirdest thing—right there in the middle of the tub was a lava rock."

Sadie turned the phone so I could see Lois. She was shaking her head, and her eyebrows were raised in astonishment. "I have no idea how that got there."

I did.

I told her and Sadie about Mom using lava rocks for her sweat ceremony. Sadie's eyes widened. Lois lifted her hand to her face and rubbed it across her lips. She started to say something and stopped.

I take that mysterious lava rock as a reminder from my mom to nourish my spirit so I have more inner space to feel joy, to be lighthearted, to walk in the world with love, to spread joy.

And in my head, I hear the words she always shared as we said goodbye:

"Have fun."

Reflection

How do you nourish your spirit so you have more inner space to feel joy?

What would JOY do?

Joy shines light on joy.

Joy shines light on joy.

Joy shines light on joy.

Joy shines light on happiness.

Four

Happiness

Happiness is when you feel your heart open, and light weaves its way in and back out and then back in again.

What fills your heart
with happiness?

Pay Attention

One of the greatest teachings I received in psychiatric nursing school was to *pay attention*. This teaching literally saved my life, on more than one occasion, when I was working in acute psychiatry. It also supports me in my writing. Every day, wherever I go, or whatever is happening, I do my best to Pay Attention, to notice the subtleties of people, places, conversations, nature, and all living beings.

In 2015, I was providing trauma training to the staff and parents of the Future 4 Nations Aboriginal Head Start preschool program in Mission, BC. At lunchtime, the children joined us, and as you can imagine, when thirty preschoolers streamed into the room, the whole energy changed. But I noticed one little guy who stood by the door, looking around, his temperament a bit more cautious than the others.

Then I saw him lock eyes with his Kookum and run right over to her. She took his face in her hands and looked at him with so much love that his whole body changed. I saw his heart fill with happiness. It made me think about what fills my heart with happiness. I kept thinking about it on my ferry ride home, and on and off for a couple of weeks.

Then, one day, I was in a meeting, and my imagination began to wander. A whole book came to me. That book was *My Heart Fills with Happiness*; not a single word has changed. I am grateful that the book was illustrated by the incredible Julie Flett and published by Orca Books in 2016.

That little book has taken on a life of its own. It has gone places and been in more classrooms, libraries, and homes than I could have ever imagined. I have read *My Heart Fills with Happiness* in well over a hundred classes across Canada and the United States, and after reading, I always do a circle with the children, asking them to share what fills their hearts with happiness. Their responses are always about relationships—the people and animals they love. Sure, some examples include a bicycle, a video game, or a movie, but those are always in relation to doing the activity with someone they love. I am constantly reminded of the importance of our presence in children's lives, not the presents.

This also extends beyond children. I know for me, it is my relationships, including my relationship with myself, that support me in feeling happiness.

If I had not been paying attention that day when the children rushed in, I would've missed that beautiful moment between grandmother and grandson. I would've missed the spark that became what is truly one of my favourite books I've written.

So, my invitation to you is to Pay Attention.

What, or who, brings a smile to your face?

Time will reveal your
next best step.

Until then,

go somewhere in nature,

do something fun,

listen to or watch
something inspiring,

be with someone who fills your
heart with happiness.

What nutrient do you need today to nourish your spirit and foster happiness?

Fresh air

Time sitting by water

A walk in nature

A visit with an Elder or wise person

A visit with a friend

Laughter

Prayer

Healthy food

A good book

A podcast

A hug

A movie that makes you laugh

Being in community

A shared a meal

Time alone

A hot bath

Silence

Listening to the birds singing

Writing in your gratitude journal

A walk in the grass barefoot

A ride on a swing

A drink of water

A nap

A cuddle with a pet

A trip to the library

Music

A drive

Sending thank-you notes

Lighting a candle

A ride on a roller coaster

Making a special meal

Being of service

Dancing

A seat in the sun

Watching baseball
(or your favourite sport)

Volunteering

Reflection

How do you nourish your spirit and foster happiness?

Smile.

That is all.

Beacons of Hope

Over the seven years Rhonda and I tried to get pregnant, my hope was tested on many occasions. As was my faith in the teaching, "All good things in their rightful time."

Around year four, Rhonda and I bought our first home, a condominium in Victoria. This was massive for me! Owning a home had always seemed impossible because my family had moved numerous times when I was a kid, including the summer we were unhoused and lived on the beach in Nelson. So perhaps you can see why buying our condo was epic for me.

A couple of years after we moved in, there was an earthquake, and everything changed. I noticed the fireplace mounting had come about half an inch away from the wall. Now, we could hear every sound the people above us made. Not long after that, we learned at our strata meeting that our building was what is commonly known as a leaky condo.

The building required significant structural repairs, and our portion of the fee was $37,000—a huge sum of money for anyone, but especially for two young women working in social services. We went to the bank to explore getting a second mortgage, but that evening we had another strata meeting where we learned there had been a reassessment, and our bill was now $57,000.

We made the difficult decision to walk away. I felt like I was reliving my dad's patterns, feeling the trauma of all my childhood moves, as well as the loss of our dream home.

At the same time, I had a minor surgery to address ovarian cysts that the doctors thought were causing our difficulty sustaining a pregnancy. I travelled to Vancouver alone to what I thought was a simple post-op follow-up appointment. So, when the doctor informed me that the only way I would be able to potentially carry a baby to term was through in vitro fertilization, I felt like I had been punched in the stomach. I knew in vitro was not financially possible for us.

I left the doctor's office and called Rhonda to

tell her the news. We had a good cry and agreed that, for now, we would pause our attempts to get pregnant.

I collected myself and started the errands I had also come to Vancouver to do. I began at Ikea and found myself in the children's section. Before I knew what I was doing, I had put two small, red chairs in my cart. As the days, weeks, and months passed, those chairs became my beacons of hope during one of the darkest periods of my life.

You know the saying, "In every storm, there is a rainbow"? Well, it took a few months, but finally, the rainbow appeared. Because of the terms of the leaky condo repair, we were able to live in our condo for six months, mortgage and rent free. We saved all that money, took our moms to Maui for a week, and were able to pay for one round of in vitro fertilization.

We had one shot.

When was the last time someone asked, "How are you?"

and you replied with "Happy"?

Next time someone asks you how you are, reply with "Happy."

Notice how you feel and how people respond.

Be a rainbow in someone's cloudy day.

Our Little Miracles

About two weeks after the fertilized embryos had been put in me for our one and only round of in vitro, I was terribly sick. Rhonda called the fertility clinic, and we were instructed to get to Vancouver asap. The next morning at the clinic, I had several tests done, and almost two litres of fluid were drained from my abdomen—a side effect of the hormones.

I was in the recovery room with Rhonda sitting beside me when Gerry came in. She was the nurse who had been with us on our seven-year journey to have a baby. She explained the test results and then added, "The last test we did was a pregnancy test."

All sound fell away, except for my heart beating in my chest.

Gerry's eyes moved from me to Rhonda, and then back to me again. "Congratulations! You girls are pregnant!"

It's odd what we remember in the moments that change our life's trajectory. I wondered whether I was dreaming, but then, out of the corner of my eye, I noticed Rhonda's jeans shaking. Slowly, I turned to look at her, hand to her mouth, tears streaming down her face. I knew then that I wasn't dreaming.

"I'll give you girls a few minutes, and then I'll be back," Gerry said. "The doctor would like to do an ultrasound."

Rhonda and I held each other, no words needed.

Later, we went for our ultrasound and heard the heartbeat of our daughter, whom we instantly loved. But Rhonda told the doctor that there were supposed to be two heartbeats—she had always believed we were going to have twins.

"Just because there are two fertilized eggs doesn't mean they will both survive," he said, and then continued, "but sometimes they are still too high in the uterus and we don't hear the heartbeat yet. If you want to come back next week, we can do another ultrasound."

A week later, we rode the ferry back to Vancouver and made our way to the clinic for another ultrasound.

Ba-boom, ba-boom!

The doctor smiled and looked at Rhonda. "You were right. There's the second heartbeat. And a strong one, that's for sure." That was our introduction to our son, whom we instantly loved.

Although we had lost our bricks-and-mortar home, we created another home. On October 7, 2003, we were blessed with an expansion of the home in our hearts—our twins, Sadie Piper and Jaxson Gray. Through them and our family, I have experienced more gratitude, love, joy, happiness, and hope than I ever could have imagined.

When Life's Pleasures Were Simple

Lying under a tree and watching
leaves twirl and swirl down
toward you.

Saturday morning cartoons.

Spending an afternoon reading.

When your only "job" was to
set the table.

Staring up at the stars and listening
to the crickets sing in harmony.

When the phone was on the wall,
and no one ever asked,
"Have you seen my phone?"

When twenty-five cents bought
you a bag full of candy at the
neighbourhood corner store.

Today's Pleasures

Clean sheet night.

Heated steering wheel on a cold winter morning.

A new journal.

The smell of coffee first thing in the morning.

An empty laundry basket.

A nap.

Freshly cut flowers.

Finding money in a jacket pocket.

Reflection

What are life's simple pleasures, past and present, that you could cultivate more of?

PLAY!

LAUGH!

Transformation

Are you familiar with the expression,
"Happiness is making lemonade
out of lemons"?

You can't turn lemons into lemonade
just by wishing for it to happen.

You must do the work to
make the change.

*

Wash

Cut

Squeeze

Squeeze some more

And, yes, squeeze some more

Add water

Add sweetener

Taste

Adjust and taste again.

*

Happiness and feeling happier don't just happen! We have to work at it. Then we might have to work at it a bit more. And along the way, we might have to adjust what makes us find happiness and feel happier. What gives us happiness today might change tomorrow, or next week.

We are always growing and evolving.

What would HAPPINESS do?

Happiness shines light
on happiness.

Happiness shines light
on happiness.

Happiness shines light
on happiness.

Happiness shines light
on hope.

Five

Hope

Hope is believing tomorrow will be better than today, and having the self-determination to make it so.

Every act of kindness is an
act of hope and light.

Hope on Pause

It was a miserable, cold, and wet Tuesday morning—a reflection of how I felt inside. I was at the acupuncturist, and he had two fingers on the inside of my wrist, taking my pulse. "It's like your hope is on pause," he said softly. A shiver rippled through my body, and tears instantly spurted from my eyes.

Sometimes the truth unleashes what we don't even realize we are holding. I was raw.

For weeks, I had been sitting each day by my dad's bedside as he was dying from cancer. And because of the pandemic, I had been unable to travel to celebrate my mom's eightieth birthday with her. My shoulders slumped, the sides of my mouth rarely rose, and a steady stream of tears flowed from my eyes.

Getting through the times when my hope is on pause has given me the deep knowing that "this too shall pass." Even if the passing isn't always on my schedule.

I've now lived long enough and had enough life experiences to know that a miserable, cold, and wet Tuesday will eventually turn into a bright and sunny Saturday.

Reflection

When in your life has it felt like your hope was on pause? How did ***you*** turn a miserable, cold, and wet Tuesday into a bright and sunny Saturday?

Hope is a muscle.

Exercise it!

Be Open.

Pay Attention.

Messages of hope
come from unexpected
people, places, and
experiences.

Believe in Possibilities

Regret, Mercy, and Hope

Regret can be the inspiration—the catalyst—we need to help us make a change so we might not feel regret again for a similar situation. Or maybe you will. Sometimes we need to learn a lesson more than once. But doing the hard work of finding the gift in regret helps soften it and turn that regret into a life learning.

Do I wish my dad had the ability to learn from his regrets earlier in his life? Sure, I do! Especially the patterns that culminated in the same or similar regrets throughout his life.

But his regrets inspired me to do some of the work he couldn't do—to change learned patterns in my family. I have different tools than he did, including starting my healing journey at the young age of twenty-two, as well as plenty of experience with Western healing and knowledge such as counselling and personal development workshops. My healing has also been rooted in Indigenous ways of healing, as well as reading, journalling, and spending time in nature. Most of these resources were not available to my dad. I am not making excuses for him; instead, I am sharing mercy, as I understand that our lived experiences and the supports we have available to help us understand ourselves today are different from my parents' generation. What is, and will be, available for my children and niece is also different.

Mercy and hope go hand in hand. Doing the work to learn from regret shines mercy on us and the situations we find ourselves in, enabling us to hope for a better future. When we give ourselves the gift of mercy, or we share mercy with another living being—human or non-human—we shine the light of hope.

Reflection

What learned family pattern do you want to change? What is one step you can take toward making that change?

All good things in their rightful time.

Stars

A few years ago, I learned that stars generate light from within. They don't need any other source to burn brightly. I want to be like a star! I want to generate light from within.

So, 'cause I'm a bit geeky about this kind of thing, I did some research. My favourite explanation for stars generating their own light was on the NASA website, where it states, "Stars are fueled by the nuclear fusion of hydrogen to form helium deep in their interiors. The outflow of energy from the central regions of the star provides the pressure necessary to keep the star from collapsing under its own weight, and the energy by which it shines."

Hope is the helium deep inside us that gives us the strength we need to ensure we do not collapse on ourselves. Hope allows us to enact the self-determination to share our shining light and brighten the world around us.

Some days I feel like my hope
is only in the cuticle of my
pinky toe,

but we must have hope!

Otherwise, we are defeated
before we even begin.

The answer is right
around the corner.

Keep going!

What would be a dream?

What would be a possibility?

What are the steps in between?

Where do you start?

Who can help?

Reflection

Find something that fosters hope—a photo, image, or object that reflects a dream or a possibility—and put it somewhere you will see it every day.

Dreams

I had a dream where I was locked in the hull of a massive container ship. It was dark, cold, and eerie. I blinked to try to adjust to the dark, but then I heard an announcement that the hull would open, and I knew the water would flood in and fill the space. I realized I would drown if I didn't find a way out. I was terrified—my legs felt like lead, my breathing was frantic, and my eyes scanned frantically for a way out. I started banging on the sides of the hull and yelling, "Help! Help! Someone, please help me!" But my pleas for help only reverberated back at me.

As I heard the metal scraping of the doors opening, I looked everywhere to find a way out. That was when I saw a small glimmer of light.

I wiped my eyes and looked again—the glimmer was still there.

I began to run, my feet sloshing in the water seeping in. The glimmer of light came from a massive door that was open just a crack. I used all my strength and pulled and pulled until that door opened enough for me to shimmy through. I took a step and fell forward onto the stairs. I pushed myself up and began climbing—climbing, climbing, climbing. With each step, the light got a bit brighter. There was hope!

Finally, I emerged in what looked like a hospital. As I collapsed, someone caught me and guided me to a bed. They removed my wet clothes and replaced them with warm pajamas. I was tucked in with the biggest and coziest duvet, definitely not the usual hospital-style thin and frayed blankets.

The person helping me said, "I will bring you some tea with honey, but for now, just rest. You are safe, there is nothing else to do but rest." And then she was gone.

My breathing began to settle, and tears of gratitude filled my eyes. Gratitude for the small glimmer of light—of hope—that kept me alive.

Take HOPE out into the world!

A Glimmer of Hope

When I was in treatment as part of my journey of recovery from alcoholism, I learned to always pay attention to my dreams as a form of guidance. I learned how the dreams we have when we first fall asleep help us heal and understand our past, the dreams we have in the middle of our sleep help us understand what is currently going on in our lives, and the dreams we have before waking up help us understand and prepare for our future.

When I woke up from that dream of being locked in the container ship, I kept replaying it in my mind, unpacking all the lessons woven within this gift. When we feel like there is only darkness, and more darkness is descending, a glimmer of light, of hope, is all we need. Sometimes we have to open that door and climb to let the light in. Sometimes someone else will open the door and help us climb to the light.

I took to heart the reminder to rest. It is rest that gives us the strength to take the next step when the time is right. But rest comes first. As we rest, light and hope nourish us.

This early-morning dream was also a reminder for me that when it feels like there is no way out of the darkness, keep searching for a glimmer up ahead.

A glimmer of hope and light.

Reflection

How often do you rest
and in what ways?

You Are a Precious Gift
and You Matter!

We are all precious.

In this world, there is
no one else like us.

No one has the same
bundle of gifts.

All eight billion of us are
precious and unique.

Sometimes we lose sight of that.

May today be a day to remember
that you are a precious gift
and you matter!

I have lots of hopes,
for you and for me,
but I wonder—
What are your hopes?

What would HOPE do?

Here's to each of us—

Being the light

Receiving the light

and

Sharing the light.

Mario Andretti Race Car Driving School

Las Vegas, September 2008

I'm not really sure where my love of driving fast came from. Maybe it's because my first car was a 1974 Toyota Corolla, and she could really go! So, when my fortieth birthday was on the horizon, I thought a lot about how I wanted to welcome that new decade into my life.

I knew Mario Andretti had a race car driving school in Las Vegas. I reached out to dear friends I wanted to celebrate this birthday with and suggested that if they wanted to send me a cheque—yes, this was back in the day of cheques—for $75 a month for the next twelve months, I would put them in an account, and at the end of the year, we would have enough money to go to Las Vegas.

A year later, we were in sunny Las Vegas, and I was at Mario Andretti's race car driving school. There were two options: drive the NASCAR race car yourself, or ride along with a professional driver. No way was I going to ride along! I wanted to be the driver of my life, not the passenger.

The first hour was a class in which we signed our lives away in waivers, acknowledging that we would not only be driving at speeds outside the normal range but also had no formal training or experience doing this.

Finally, it was time to get on the racetrack. We started by driving around the track in a van, while the instructors told us about the skirt, the side of the racetrack where we could drive, where we couldn't drive, the driver who would be our pilot car, and what different flags meant—and then it was time.

We put on flame protective suits—that should've been my first clue. Then, we put on helmets and got behind the wheel. After a short orientation about the car, I was told to follow the lead car. I had purchased fifteen laps. We did the first few laps and quickly got up to 120 miles an hour, which is about 193 kilometres an hour. I was having a hard time keeping up with the lead car.

I was afraid. I was beyond afraid—I was terrified.

When it was evident I was afraid to go faster, they gave me the flag to pull over. I followed my lead car into the pit and the driver came over and motioned for me to lower my window. "You can't be looking where you're going. You can't even really be looking at the next corner." He pointed up the track. "We're going way too fast for you to only be looking where you're going. You will crash." He paused for a moment, letting the instruction sink in. "And we don't want that." I shook my head from side to side. "You have to imagine where you want to be going and how you will get there. You have to be able to see it in your mind's eye, and then you can make it happen."

A powerful lesson for the racetrack—and life!

My lead driver leaned further into the window and added, "You're doing good, but not good enough."

I had to look away because those words made my throat clench and my breath catch. They reminded me of how my dad used to speak to me, saying I did good, but the way he said it always left me feeling like I never did good enough. This message from my dad about not being good enough had haunted me for most of my life.

The next laps were an opportunity to leave behind that feeling of not being good enough. Not for anyone else's standards, but for me. For me to begin to honestly design who and how I wanted to be in the world, without an inner voice saying I wasn't good enough to be in the driver's seat.

In my final laps, I reached 150 miles an hour, which is about 240 kilometres an hour. I felt exhilarated!

And when we pulled back into the pit, I also knew I never needed to drive that fast again.

That day, I let go of the feeling of not being good enough, though it occasionally still rears its head. I also learned an important lesson about visioning. About not looking at where I'm going, but rather at what I want to create around the corner. About how to envision my goals, hopes, dreams, and possibilities before I can actually see them. This requires a delicate balance between being present in the here and now *and* taking time to envision what I want to experience and bring into the world. I continually ask myself: "What do I want to dream and speak into the future?"

As we come to a close, what are your hopes and dreams for the future? And how will you make them happen?

This is as much of a reminder for me as for you—practise, practise, and practise some more. Intentionally practise the five ways of being: gratitude, love, joy, happiness, and hope. As you've probably heard, "practice makes perfect." Well, we aren't looking for perfection, but we are looking to generate the light that practice can give us.

If I had been practising driving that race car on the Vegas track for the previous fifteen years, well, perhaps driving 200 miles an hour would have felt comfortable, familiar, safe. The practices in this book are like that—with regular and frequent use, they become more natural. Then, they become part of your routine to embrace your light and share it with the world.

Love,

Monique

Hope shines light on hope.

Hope shines light on hope.

Hope shines light on hope.

Hope shines light on gratitude,

love,

joy,

happiness,

and more

HOPE.

Reflection

Take a moment and return to the beginning of this book when I spoke of the hummingbird. What messages, ideas, or insights are you taking away with you?

Gratitude opens the doors for goodness and grace.

Love is medicine.

Joy is in the seemingly small, day-to-day moments in life.

Happiness is when you feel your heart open, and light weaves its way in and back out and then back in again.

Hope is believing the future will be better than today, and having the self-determination to make it so.

Permissions

"Fill a Room with Love," *Tilly: A Story of Hope and Resilience*, Monique Gray Smith, Sono Nis Press, 2013.

"Letters from Love—with Special Guest Monique Gray Smith!" Elizabeth Gilbert's Substack, September 24, 2023, elizabethgilbert.substack.com/p/letters-from-love-with-special-guest-f4f?utm_source=publication-search.

Braiding Sweetgrass: Indigenous Wisdom, Scientific Knowledge, and the Teachings of Plants, Robin Wall Kimmerer, Milkweed Editions, 2015.

I Hope, Monique Gray Smith, illustrated by Gabrielle Grimard, Orca Book Publishers, 2022.

Acknowledgements and Appreciations

To my wife, Rhonda, thank you for always believing in me, my ideas, and my books way before I do. Thank you for all the ways you take care of me and our family.

To my children, Jaxson and Sadie, you have and continue to bring more light and love to my life than you may ever know... You are my most precious gifts.

To my sister, Teresa, I am grateful for our Saturday morning breakfasts, our walks at the lagoon, our laughs, our tears, and for all the light you share with me and the world.

To my initial readers, Rhonda Peterson, Teresa Dobmeier, Shannon Lundquist, Robin Ducharme,

Anne Marie Hogya, Kelly Terbasket, Shelagh Rogers, and Margo D'archangelo, my hands are raised to each of you. Your feedback, curiosities, and suggestions have helped shape this book. Each of you, in your own way, has a special place in my heart.

To Shambu and Nicole, both of you have been integral to my healing and wellness, as well as my journey with grief. Thank you for sharing your gifts, wisdom, rituals, and light with me. I am immensely grateful.

Deep gratitude to Semareh Al-Hillal for seeing the potential of and believing in this book.

I am grateful for my editor, Shirarose Wilensky! Your ability to edit with love and kindness helped me to go deeper into each and every story. Without you, this book may still be embedded in my computer.

To my agent, Jacqui Lipton, I appreciate you! Thank you for always being my advocate and for sharing our desire for a kinder and more loving world.

And to you, the reader, thank you for going on this journey with me and for sharing your light with the world.

The facts about stars are from the NASA website, science.nasa.gov/astrophysics/focus-areas/how-do-stars-form-and-evolve/.

MONIQUE GRAY SMITH is an award-winning, bestselling author for children and adults and an accomplished international speaker and consultant. She is of Cree and Scottish descent and has been sober and on her healing journey for more than thirty-four years. Her debut novel, *Tilly: A Story of Hope and Resilience*, won the 2014 Burt Award for First Nations, Métis and Inuit Literature. Monique and her family are blessed to live on the traditional territory of the WSÁNEĆ people near Victoria, British Columbia.